B. Reigns

# B. Reigns, Shanthamani. M and M. Thébault at Gallery Sumukha, Bangalore — India
## December 9th 2017 — 31st January 2018

B. Reigns

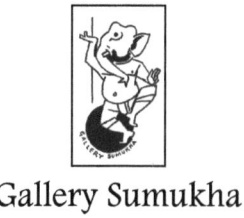

Gallery Sumukha

B. Reigns was an exhibit with Bamboo as
its medium. Bamboo as a material is eco-
friendly and self-sustainable. Not many
artists have worked with it, so I was very
fascinated to see the outcome of the works.
Shanthamani and Marc come from diverse
artistic and cultural sensibilities; it was
very interesting to see how differently they
perceived the local material.

My gallery is a platform for established
and next generation artists to showcase
all forms and media of contemporary art.
We support artists in terms of commissions
and relevant spaces to expose their
conceptual thinking, thus marking it as an
international space. Simultaneously we
present Indian contemporary artists, abroad
through exhibitions and participation in
International Art Fairs.

Gallery Sumukha — Bengaluru was
established in 1996 and has evolved over
the years. It is currently housed in the
largest private gallery space of South India.
We cater to a wide audience, nationally
and internationally, and have a history of
working with external curators and artists
from various parts of the world.

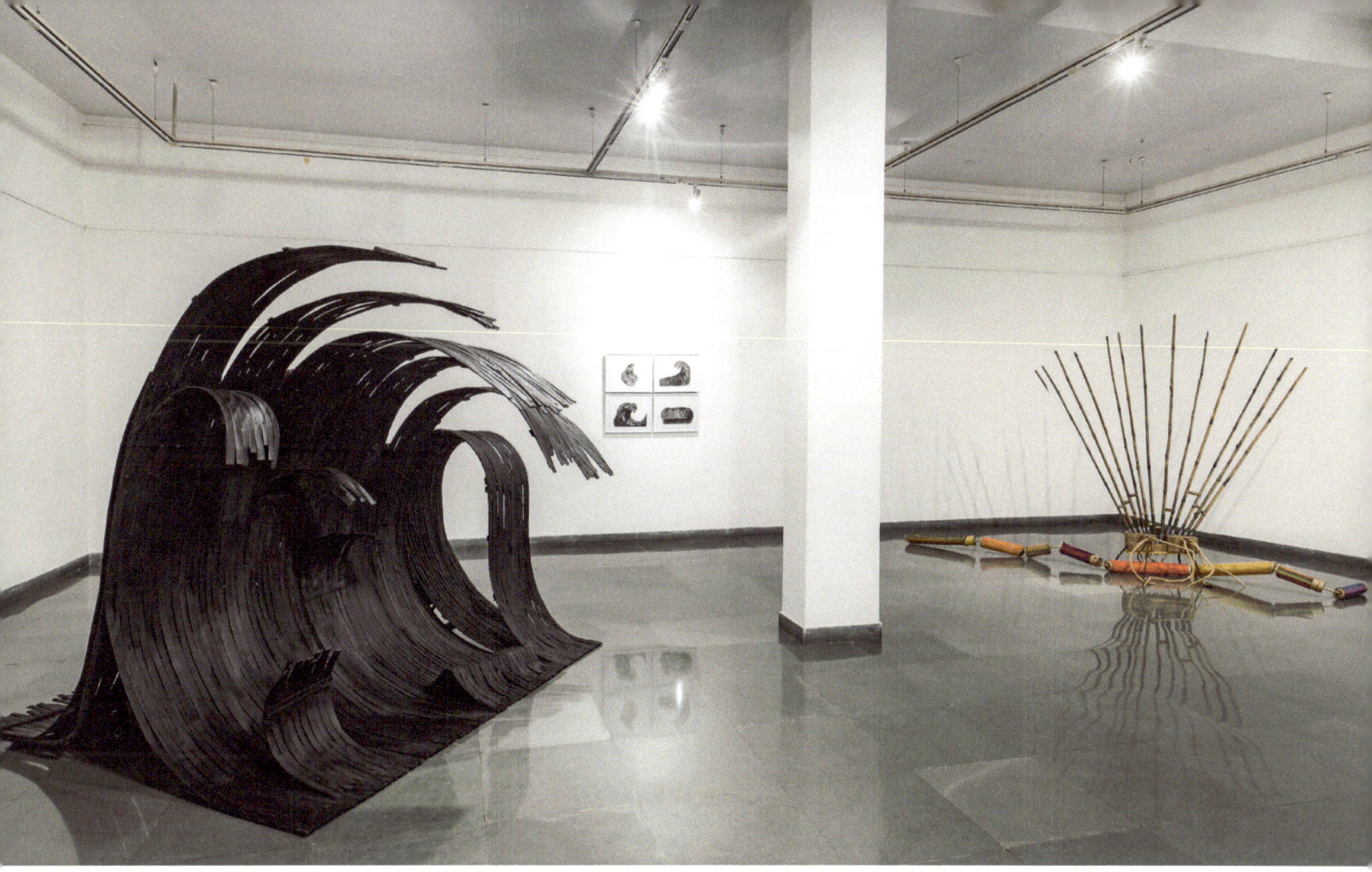

Exploring, analyzing and adapting bamboo as a material for art production, and propagating its use in our lives with a strong scientific and eco-politically correct stance is what makes this exposition vital and relevant. Shanthamani. M and Marc Thébault, taking a cue from the traditional architecture of Karnataka, underline the synonyms of the material — medium and message — that they have chosen through their works.

Here, the versatile material bamboo, that has been used for food, for making architecture, furniture and several other things for ages in Asia, is finding its way into art with a sharp conceptual and social edge. Manipulating a material for art means experimenting its potential with all freedom of imagination. The result of such an enquiry slowly permeates into the knowledge system related to that medium. In this case, the strength, pliability, verticality, sustainability, eco-friendliness and the short-term yield of it bamboo enables us in its uninterrupted availability for fuel are being brought onto an intellectual plane and it kindles our imagination to make further research and examination on the veracity of the results.

Artistically, this collaboration has also helped the artists to bring out diverse dimensions of their visual imagination based on a single material. While the lyrical and linear visual language of Marc contrasts with the robust and organic forms of Shanthamani, our visual experience becomes more energetic and of deeper involvement.

Shanthamani Muddaiah

As a contemporary artist working across
the borders of a variegation of cultures,
it becomes important to create forms and
images that can lend themselves to the
complex geopolitical intricacies of our time;
and as a woman awash in the specificity
of culture of my location — where being
a woman has severe implications — I wanted
to acknowledge the body and imbibe
my thought process in a physical form.
Therefore, the coming together of matter
and material itself becomes a part of
the exuded statement.

The element of carbon manifests in a
variety of roles in our life cycles — as carbon
life generating progress with carbon fuel,
our mega metropolises serve as safe havens
to contemplate the threat of global warming.
The very existence of life on earth is
threatened by carbon monoxide and we
cling to our carbon filters to breathe
our air. Through my journey of understanding
the material, my art embodies themes
of preserving hope and identifying
fresh solutions, rather than catering to its
aesthetic duties.

Wood-charcoal is a form of carbon that
is popularly used in India as fuel for cooking —
it entails fragments of burnt wood, not
yet completely obsolete but in a transitive
stage — a surprisingly topical allegory to life
in dense urban environments — exhausted
but caught in between.

Extending similar concerns, bamboo /
bamboo charcoal is also a material in the
spotlight as a sustainable solution for basic
human lifestyle requirements. In some
parts of India, people eat, live and sustain
their livelihoods entirely off bamboo because
of how quickly it can replenish itself.
I believe that it is of critical importance
to understand and adapt to this material
for development — in the lens of sustainable
growth as well as in order to preserve the
ecological balance of our forests.

My work in this show, inspired by traditional
practices and forms, bears motifs of our
ecological surroundings, contemporary
sensibilities and other issues. Comprising
a number of layers alluding to various
spheres of life, the work allows for analysis
in multiple perspectives.

Marc Thébault

French artist Marc Thébault came to
Bengaluru from his home in France
to collaborate with Bengaluru based artist
Shanthamani Muddaiah to transform
bamboo into contemporary art sculptures
for the exhibition B. Reigns at Gallery
Sumukha Bengaluru.

Thébault is interested in landscapes,
the spaces we inhabit and the emotional
effects these environments have on our
wellbeing. He takes the natural materials
in the environment he is working/living
in as a starting point for his art practice.
To begin work on B. Reigns, it was essential
for Thébault to visit Shanthamani's studio
in Bengaluru, to get a sense of the place
and connect on an emotional level.

He was struck by the emotional response
he felt on encountering the terrace, the
vegetation, the lake and changing light
throughout the day. This landscape had a
similar impact on Thebault to the emotions
he feels when encountering the light,
rocks and water of his hometown of Brittany,
France.

A new experience for Thébault was the presence of wild animals in the immediate environment and this also influenced his work as can be seen in B veg Reign. As is usual for Thébault, he has combined several materials in the making of these forms and so, along with using bamboo to create the pieces, Thebault also used specific stones from the area such as marble from Rajasthan, Mysore soapstone and a stone found on the path outside the studio.

It was important for Thébault that the sculptural forms are seen first rather then the bamboo, so he has added colourful threads of cotton to the outside of the bamboo. The thread is produced by DMC in Mulhouse, France where Thebault has his studio. It was the only material he brought with him from France for the project. B minReign is a simple architectural form, similar in form to the ruins of an old Greek temple. Green thread has been used on the uprights calling to mind how vegetation takes over when buildings are abandoned by humans.

For Thébault the use of sustainable materials such as bamboo and other natural materials in the production of artworks, instead of plastic or steel, is hugely important as it is up to each of us to take responsibility in caring for our planet.

Exhibition view     Gallery Sumukha     Shanthamani. M     *Carbon Wave*
                    Bangalore                                Burnt bamboo,
                                                             cane, paint
                                                             & metal
                                                             93 x 90 x 78 in.
                                                             Work executed
                                                             with technical
                                                             support of
                                                             Bamboopecker

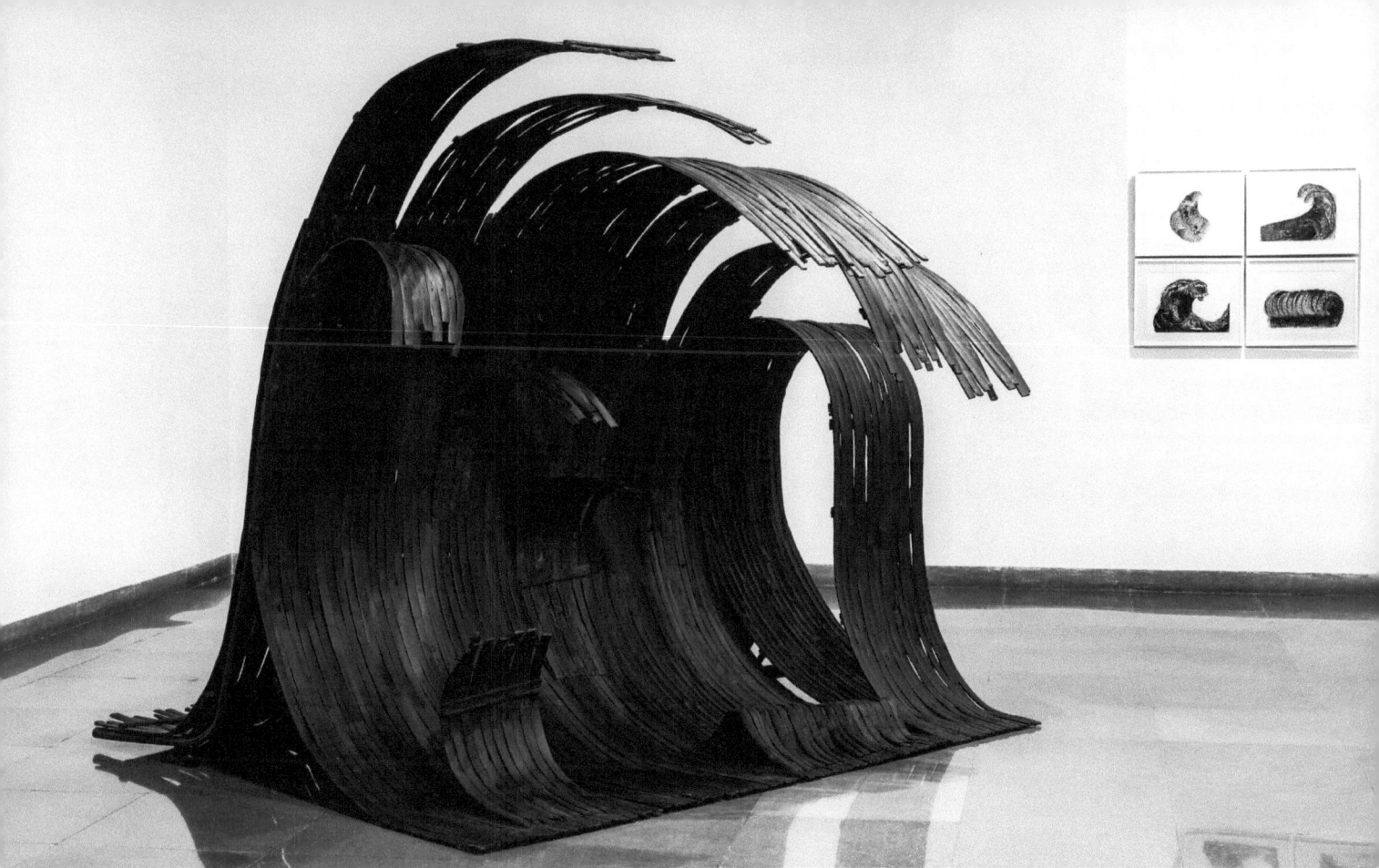

B. Reigns                                                    15

Exhibition view

Gallery Sumukha
Bangalore

Shanthamani. M

*Carbon Wave*
Burnt bamboo,
cane, paint
& metal
93 x 90 x 78 in
Work executed
with technical
support of
Bamboopecker

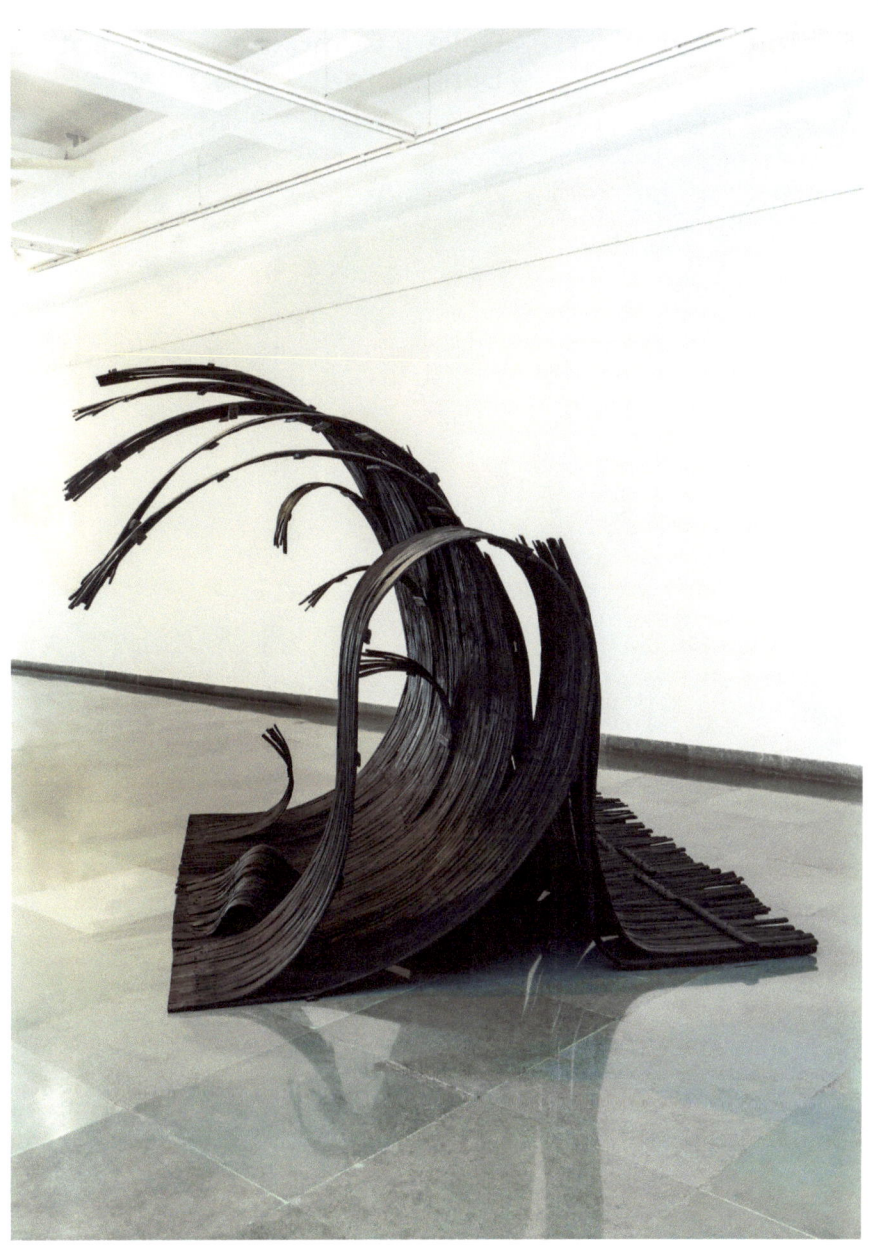

Exhibition view     Gallery Sumukha     Shanthamani. M     *Drop/Argya*
                    Bangalore                                Burnt bamboo,
                                                             cane, paint
                                                             & metal
                                                             68 x 68 x 80 in

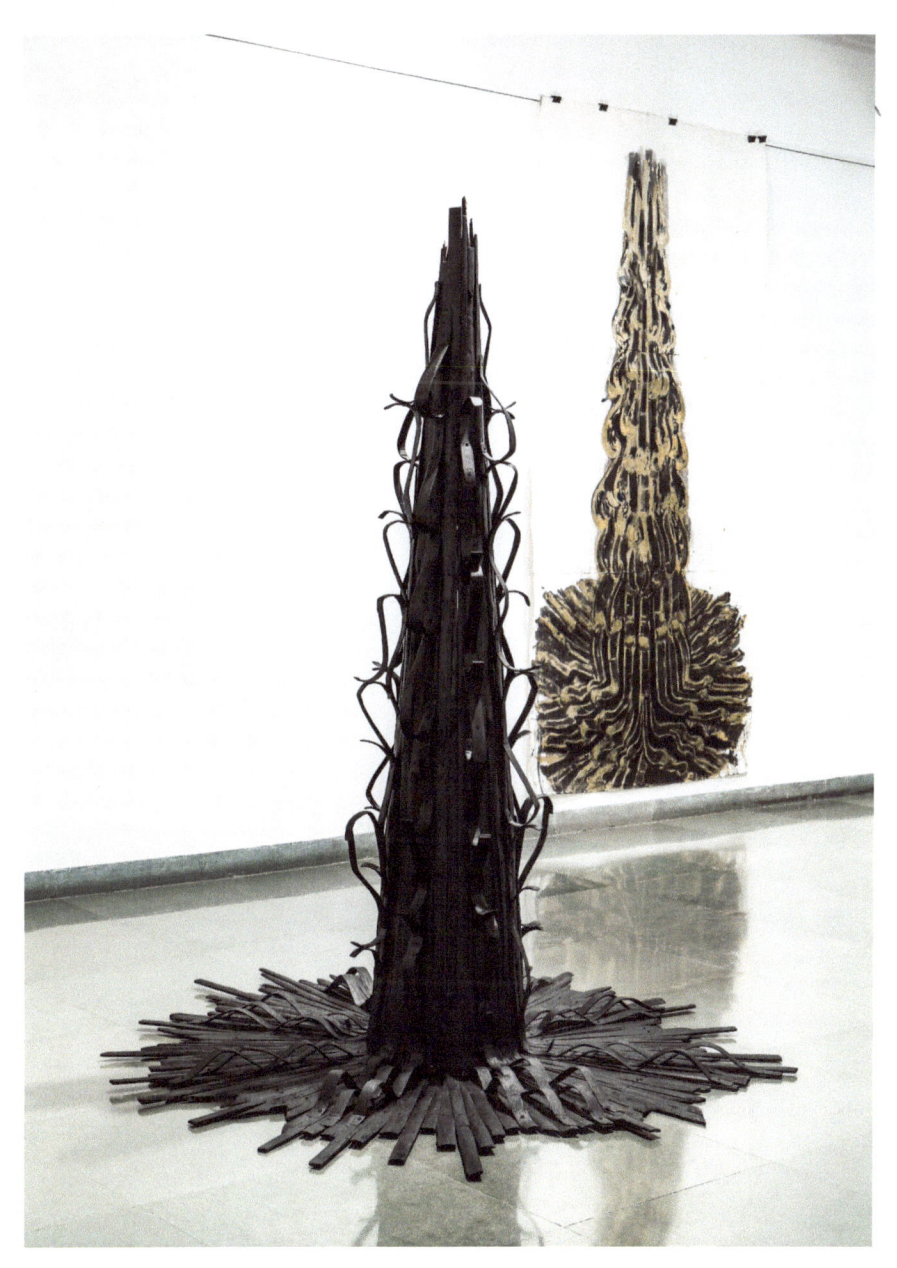

Exhibition view    Gallery Sumukha
                   Bangalore

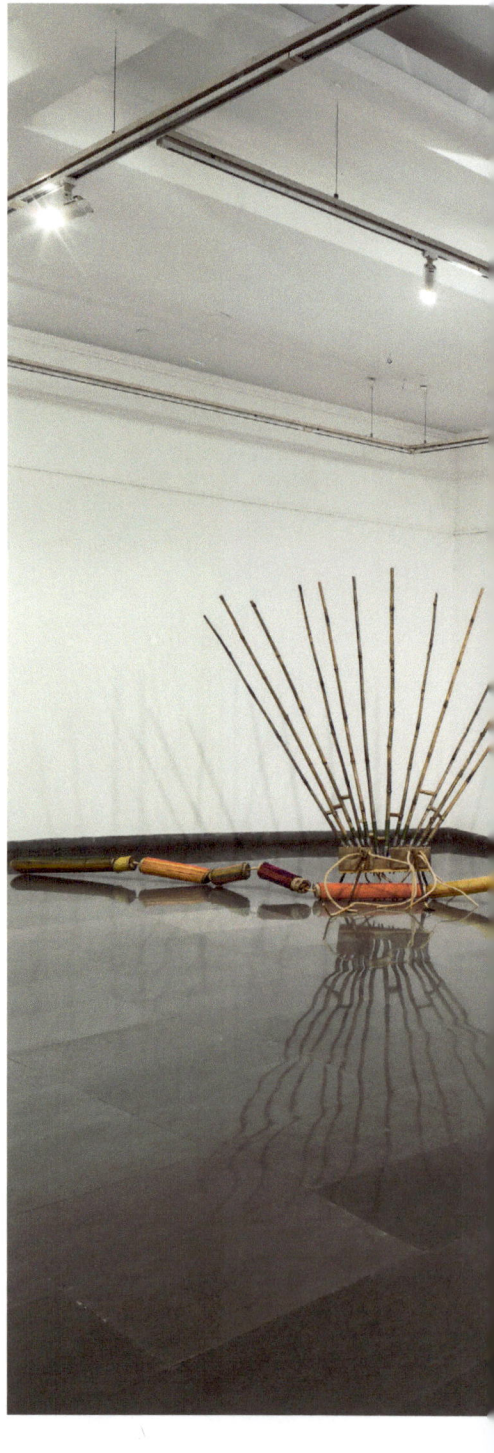

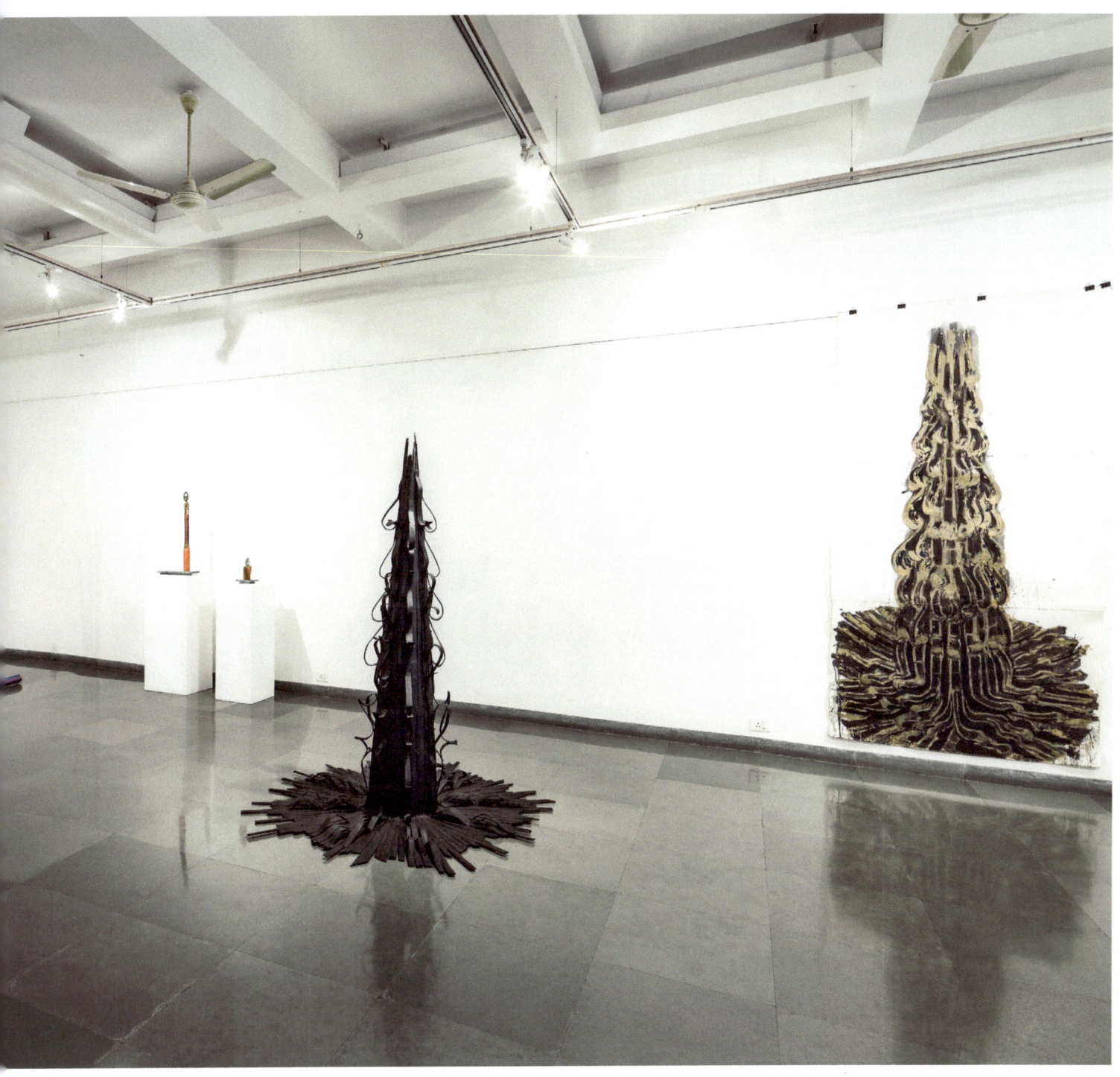

B. Reigns

Exhibition view       Gallery Sumukha       M. Thébault       *B veg Reigns*
                      Bangalore                               Bamboo,
                                                              cotton, wood
                                                              143 x 51 x 88 in

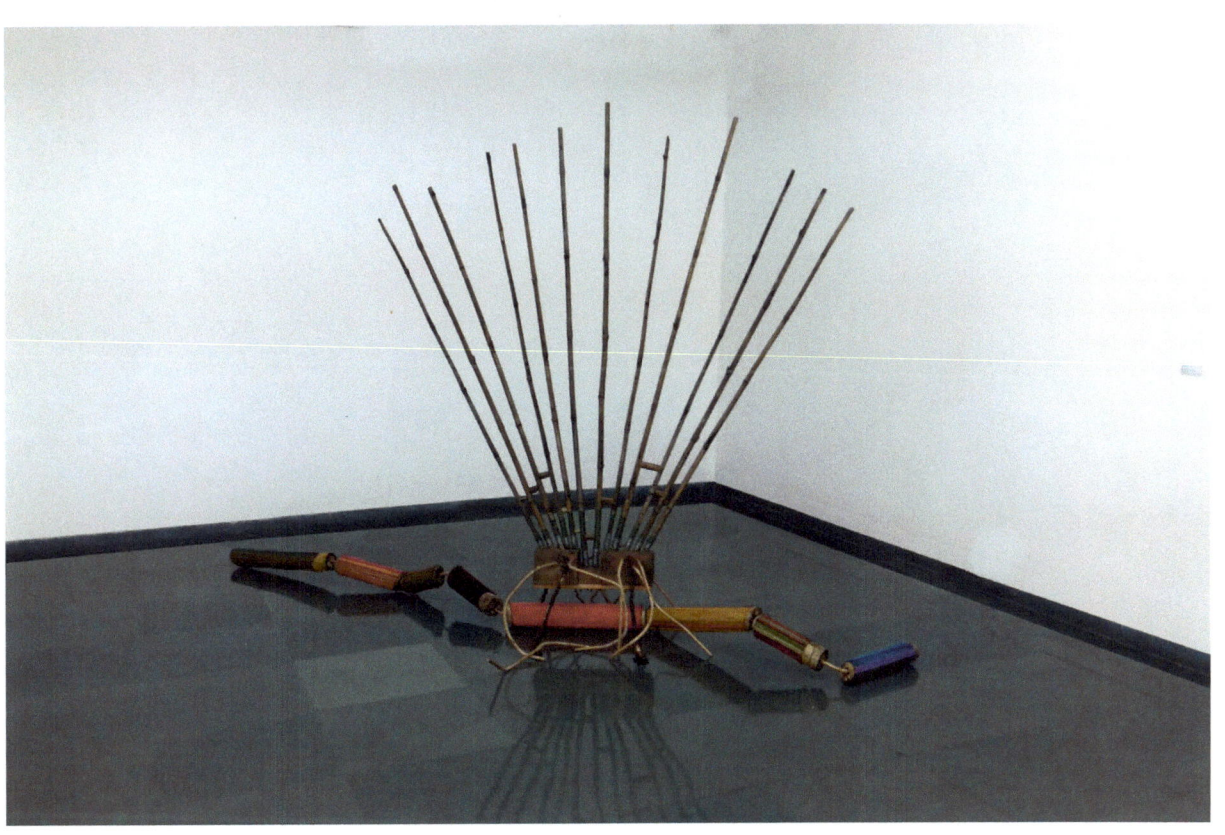

Exhibition view          Gallery Sumukha          M. Thébault          *B telscopReign*
                         Bangalore                                     Bamboo,
                                                                       cotton threads
                                                                       & stone
                                                                       16 x 6 x 30 in

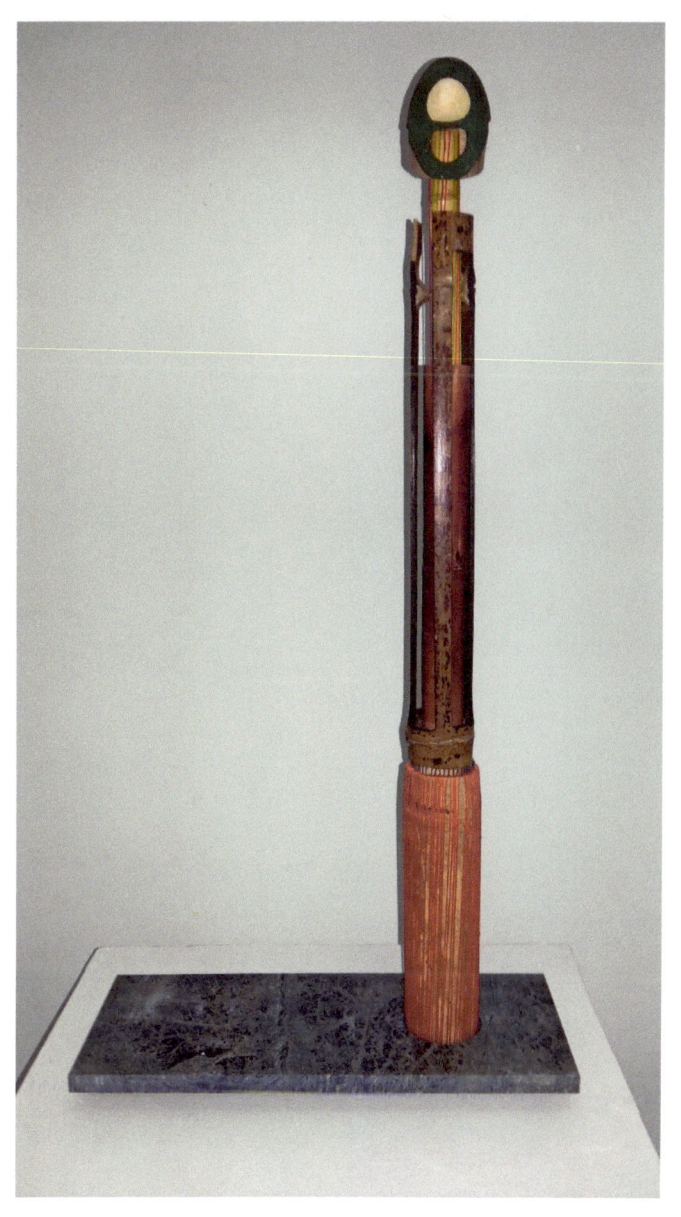

B. Reigns                                25

Exhibition view
Gallery Sumukha
Bangalore

M. Thébault

*B shoot Reign*
Bamboo,
cotton threads
& stone
6 x 6 x 10 in

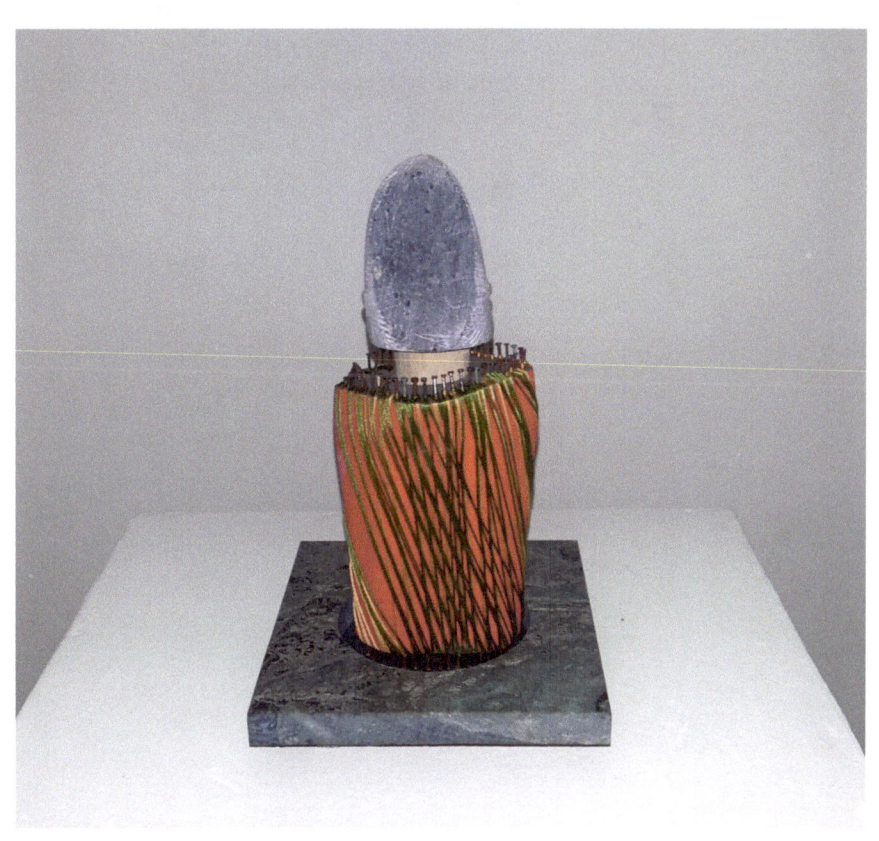

Exhibition view     Gallery Sumukha
                    Bangalore

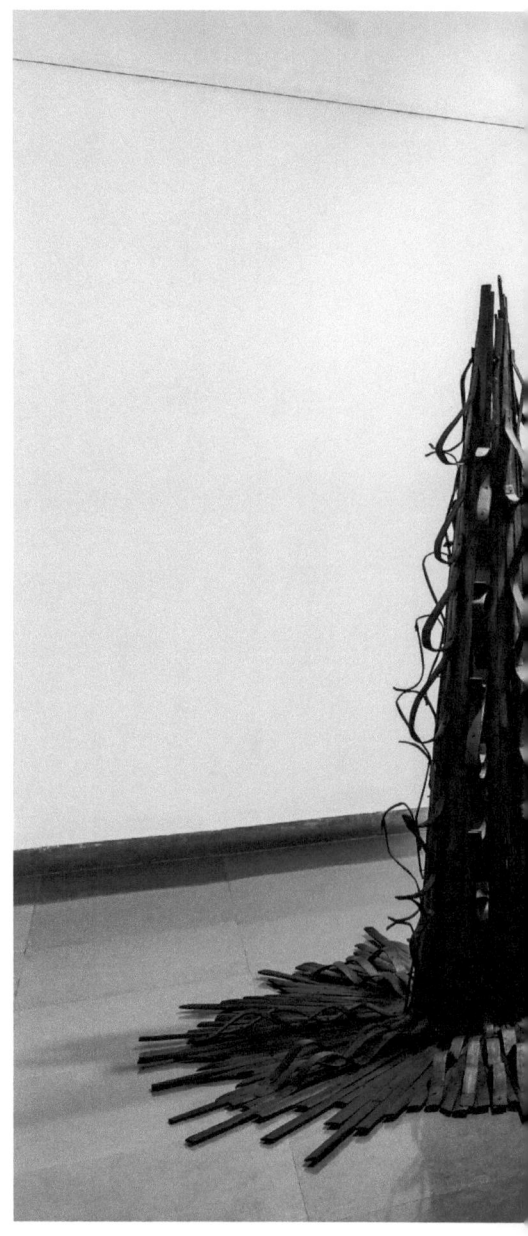

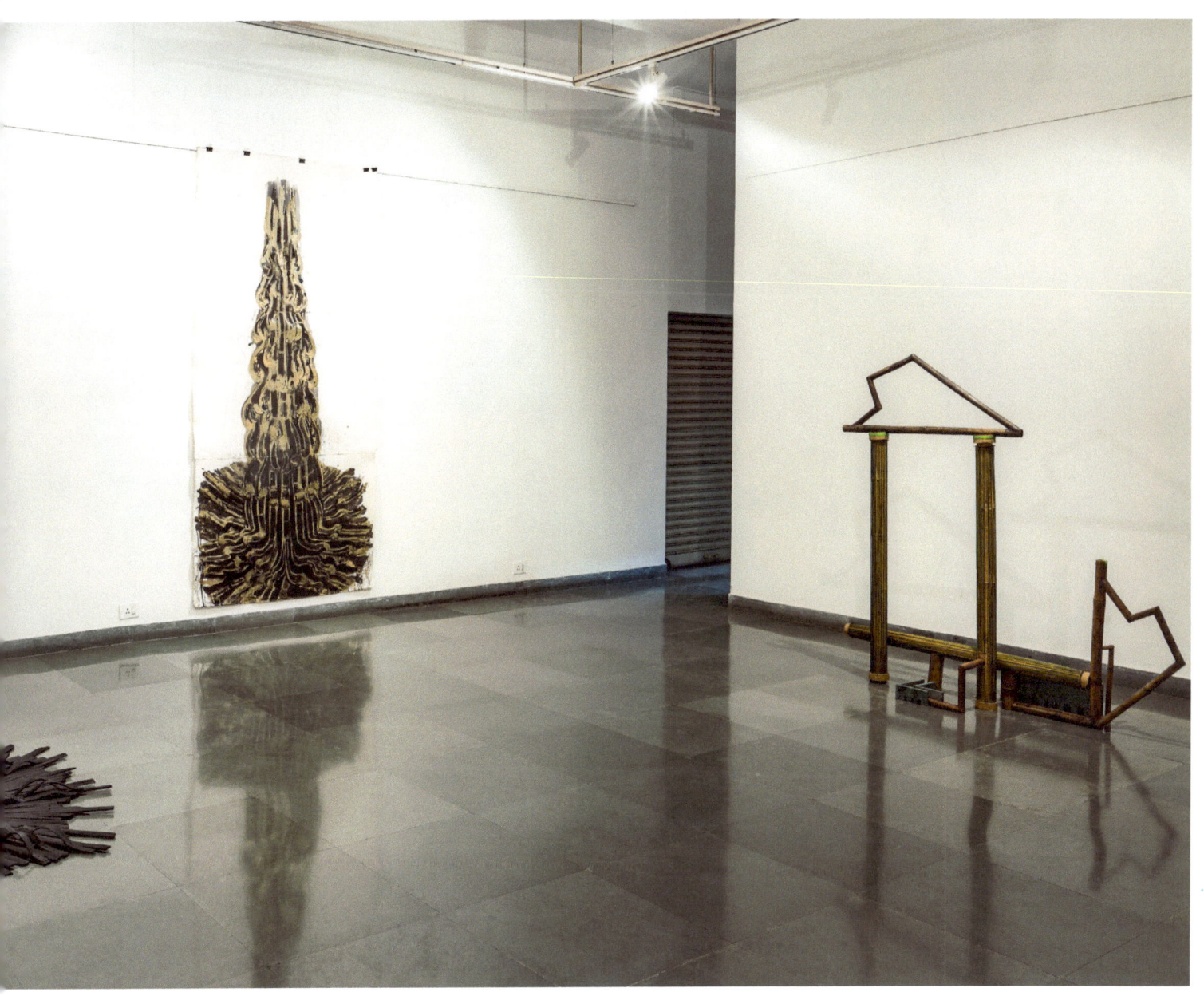

B. Reigns

Exhibition view

Gallery Sumukha
Bangalore

M. Thébault

*B min Reign*
Bamboo,
cotton threads
& stone
65 x 19 x 66 in

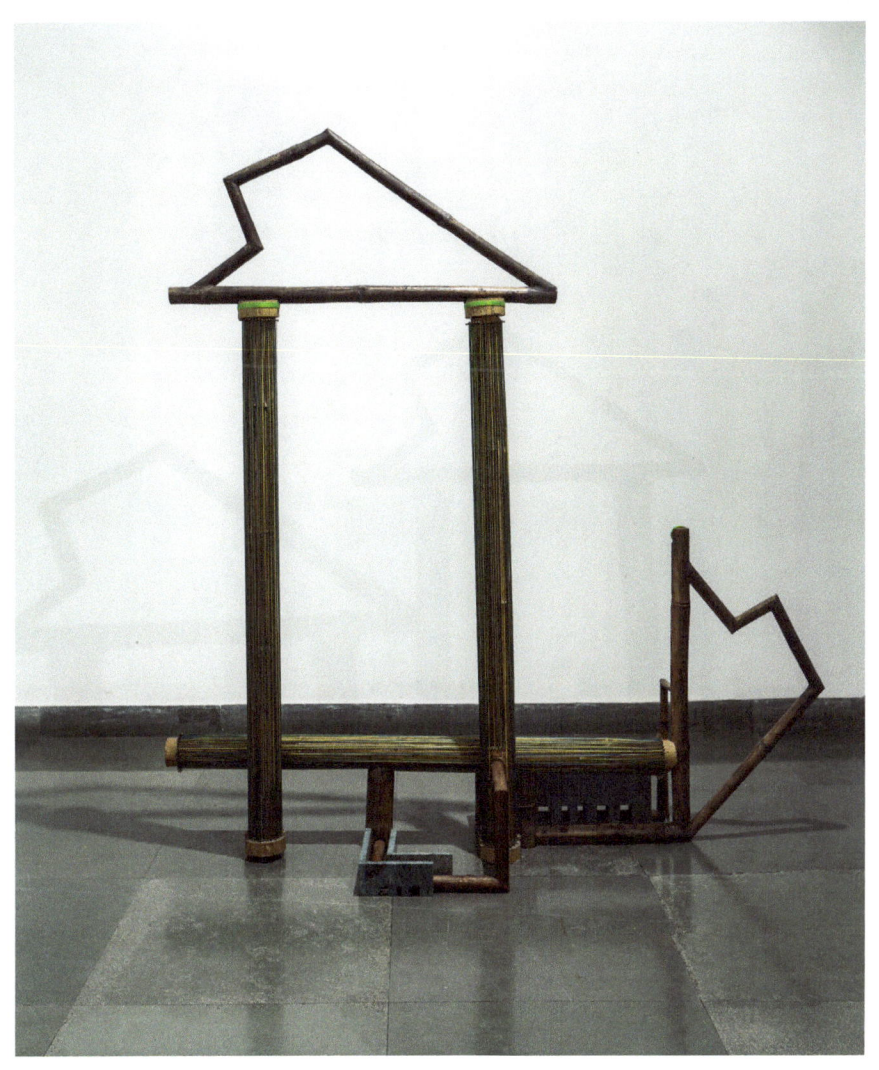

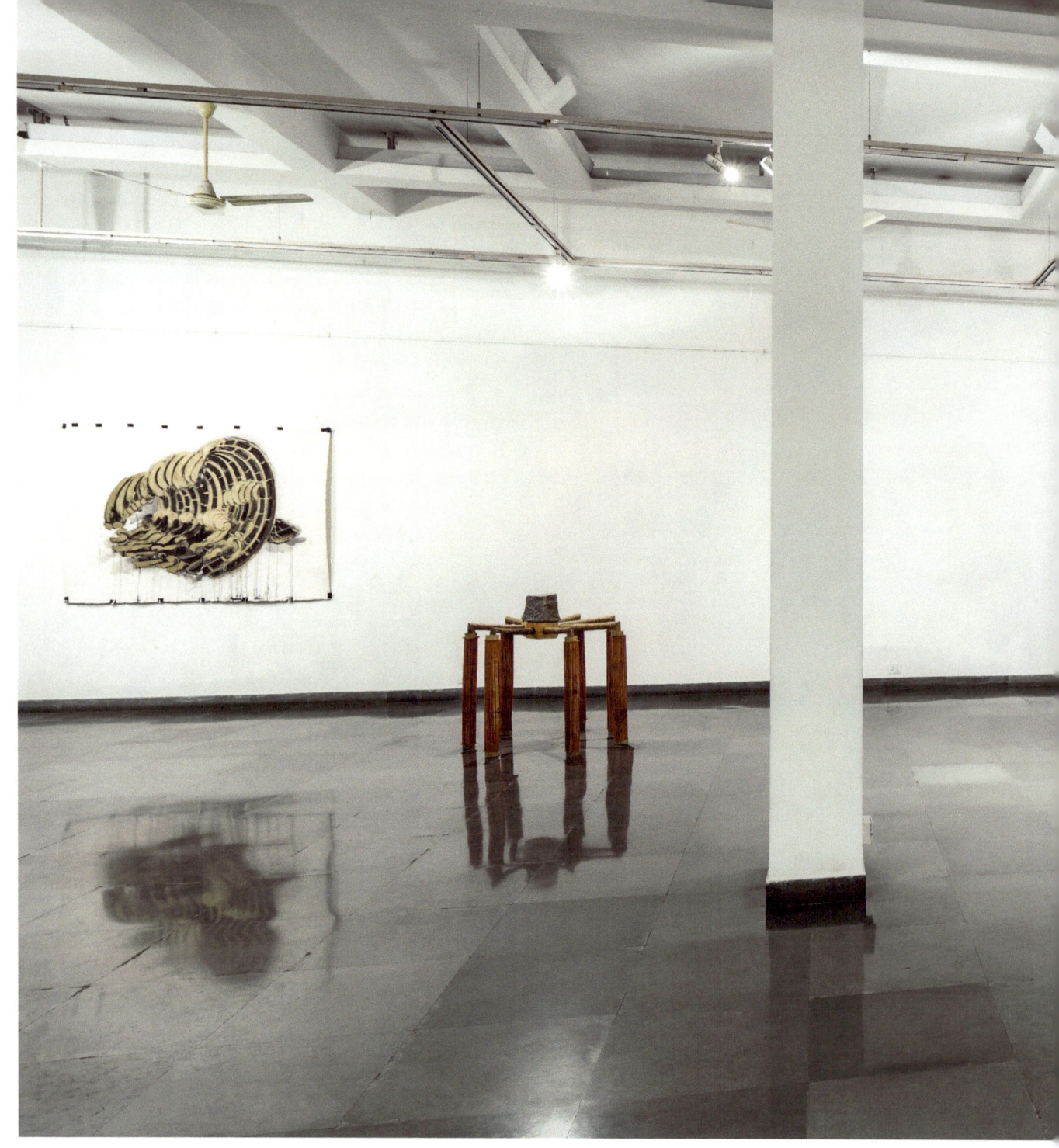

B. Reigns

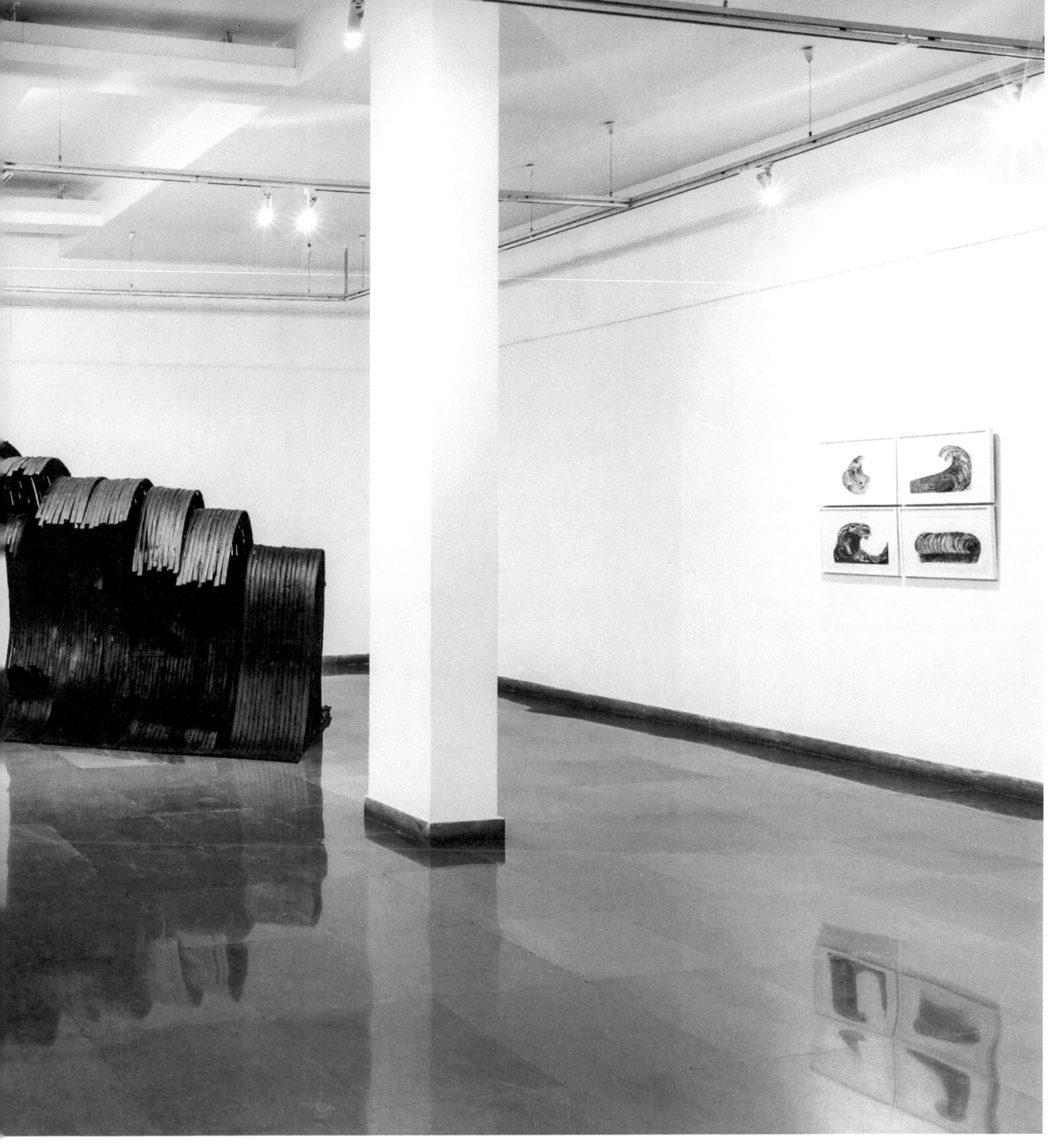

Exhibition view

Gallery Sumukha
Bangalore

M. Thébault

*B aniReign*
Bamboo,
cotton threads
& stone
40 x 40 x 39 in

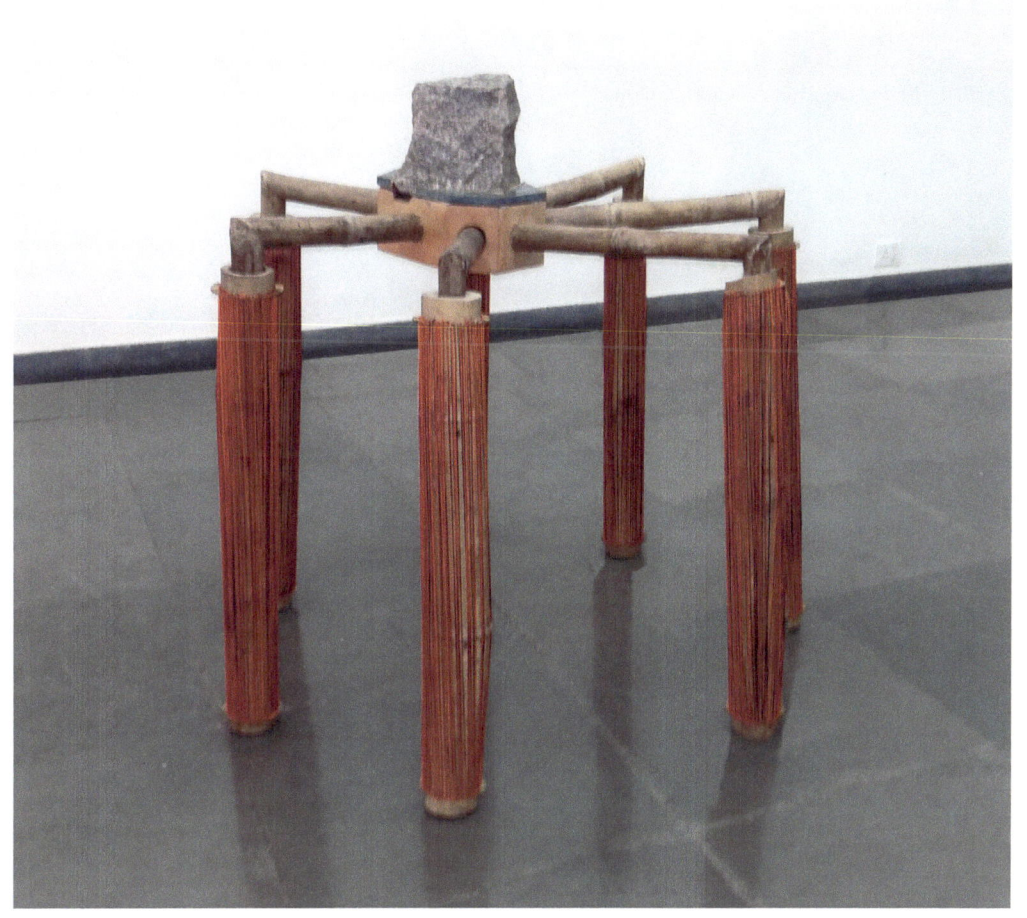

B. Reigns